A Day in the Life of a COWHAND

Diana Herweck

Consultant

Timothy Rasinski, Ph.D.
Kent State University

Curt Brummet
Cowboy

Publishing Credits

Dona Herweck Rice, *Editor-in-Chief*

Robin Erickson, *Production Director*

Lee Aucoin, *Creative Director*

Conni Medina, M.A.Ed., *Editorial Director*

Jamey Acosta, *Editor*

Heidi Kellengerger, *Editor*

Lexa Hoang, *Designer*

Lesley Palmer, *Designer*

Stephanie Reid, *Photo Editor*

Rachelle Cracchiolo, M.S.Ed., *Publisher*

Based on writing from *TIME For Kids*.

TIME For Kids and the *TIME For Kids* logo are registered trademarks of TIME Inc. Used under license.

Teacher Created Materials

5301 Oceanus Drive
Huntington Beach, CA 92649-1030
http://www.tcmpub.com
ISBN 978-1-4333-3649-2
© 2012 Teacher Created Materials, Inc.

Table of Contents

"Yee-haw!" yell the cowhands as they race off to round up the cattle. It's early in the morning, and their day is already beginning. There's so much to do!

THE FIRST COWHANDS

When people first started keeping large herds of cattle, or cows and bulls, they needed a way to keep them together. In Mexico, there were **vaqueros** (vah-KAIR-ohz) as early as the 1500s. Vaqueros were the first cowhands. They herded the cows and bulls. They did most of their work on horseback.

▼ Horses have always been important in the life and work of a cowhand.

Some cowhands work from sunup to sundown. Before the sun rises, the cowhands start their day by putting on the right clothes. These can include **chaps**, boots, spurs, a **bandana**, and a hat. Chaps and boots are used to protect the cowhand's legs and ankles while riding through cactus and brush. Spurs may look dangerous, but they are not meant to hurt a horse.

◄ hat

▶ bandana

LEATHER

Cowhand boots and chaps are made of leather so they can't be torn when the cowhands ride through thorny areas. The boots have high, slanted heels to help keep a cowhand's feet from slipping through the stirrups.

chaps ▶

Instead, the horse is urged on by a gentle tap to its ribs from the spurs attached to the cowhand's boots.

Bandanas and hats are used to protect the cowhand's face and neck from the wind, rain, and sun. Bandanas can also be used as a washcloth for the cowhand to clean things, or to cover the eyes of a scared horse.

▼ spur

FAVORITE TOOL

A **lariat** is a long rope used to catch horses, cattle, or other livestock. It is also called a lasso.

Once they are dressed for the day, the cowhands have a hearty breakfast before heading out. They need all the energy they can get to round up the cattle.

▲ A cowhand's work is hard to do, so it's important to start the day with a good breakfast.

cowhands
using lariats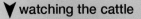

watching the cattle

NAME GAME

Cowhands in different regions are called by different names. There are vaqueros in the south. Cowhands in the north are called *buckaroos*. In Australia, they are called *drovers* or *jackaroos* (*jillaroos* for women). It wasn't until the 1860s that the word **cowboy** came into common use. Today, we sometimes say "cowhand" or "cowboy" and "cowgirl" because both men and women can do the job.

Cowhands on the Range

After breakfast, the cowhands head out on the **range** to round up and care for the cattle. They gather the animals that have wandered away from the ranch. During the roundups, a team of cowhands fans out on the plains and brings the cattle together. This is called a **cattle drive**.

In a cattle drive, **point riders** lead the herd. **Swing men** work the middle of the herd, and **drag men** are at the rear.

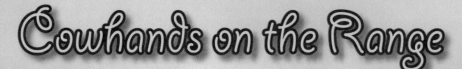

BARBED WIRE

Cattle tend to wander around if they are not fenced in. Long ago, fences were expensive and not strong enough to keep the cattle inside. Cowhands had to cover hundreds of miles to herd a rancher's cows. When barbed wire was invented in 1874, ranchers could fence off their land cheaply. So, cowhands are needed to cover fewer miles.

MODERN TIMES

Long ago, cattle drives lasted for months as cattle were moved long distances to be sold. It doesn't usually happen that way anymore. Today, big trucks move cattle long distances, and helicopters can be used to search for cattle that have wandered away. Even so, there are still cattle drives and roundups on ranches, and many cowhands still do their work on horseback, just as they did long ago.

All of the cowhands work together to keep the cattle moving, even the slow or injured ones.

While they herd cattle, cowhands rope the young calves in order to brand them and give them medical care. It may take three or four cowhands to work with one calf.

As one cowhand ropes the calf by the horns, another will rope him by the legs, pulling him to the ground. One or two cowhands then **brand**, **ear tag**, and **immunize** the calf.

ear tags on cattle ➤

MEDICAL CARE

Shots immunize calves and other animals from illness. People can receive immunizations, too. An ear tag is a marker to label cattle. Some ear tags also have medicine to protect the cattle from insects.

some examples of brands ➤

▲ Cowhands must work together to brand the cattle.

CATTLE BRANDING

Each ranch has a brand that makes a scar on the cattle. The scar, or brand, is made to identify the owner of the cattle. It is made with a hot **branding iron.** People have been branding their animals for thousands of years. There is even an Egyptian tomb from 2,000 B.C. that shows a branding scene!

The cowhands also **dehorn** the calves. They use a **scoop**, which cuts the horns down to stumps. Dehorning protects the cattle from hurting one another during travel. It also keeps them from gouging (GOUJ-ing), or stabbing, the cowhands with their sharp horns.

At midday, cowhands stop for lunch. A cook sets up the **chuck wagon** so he or she can fix the meal. The cook makes a quick lunch so the cowhands can get back to herding the cattle. There's still a lot of work to do.

DID YOU KNOW?

There is a National Cowgirl Museum in Texas. The museum honors women who demonstrate bravery and independence. Visitors can attend Cowgirl University and learn roping and riding skills, as well as ranch skills.

FOOD ON THE RANGE

The cook brings lots of food when the cowhands are out on the range. This usually includes beef, beans, bacon, bread, canned milk, flour, dried fruit, and coffee.

After working hard all morning, cowhands are very hungry. ∨

Cowhands spend the rest of the afternoon as they did the morning. They round up and care for the cattle.

While they work, the cowhands are careful not to **startle** the cattle. If cattle get scared, they run and scatter. This is called a **stampede.** It can take hours to gather and calm them and get them back on the trail.

Before the cowhands settle in for the night, they care for their horses. The horses have worked hard all day, too. The cowhands remove their horses' saddles, feed them, and release them onto the open range to relax.

The cowhand's work is tiring, so it feels good to relax at the end of the day.

The cowhands prepare a campfire, eat, and tell stories. They play cards, sing songs, and get some sleep. They need to be ready to get up bright and early the next morning, sometimes as early as three o'clock. Cowhands often rise before the sun!

A COWHAND'S DAY

A cowhand's day might look something like this.

3:00 A.M.	Wake up, get dressed, take care of the horses, and eat breakfast.
4:00 A.M.	Saddle up and head out on the range to work the cattle.
5:00 A.M.	Herd the cattle and tend to the calves.
11:00 A.M.	Stop for lunch at the chuck wagon.
12:00 P.M.	Get back to work herding cattle.
5:00 P.M.	Care for the horses and settle in for the night.
6:00 P.M.	Eat dinner at the chuck wagon.
6:30 P.M.	Relax with the other cowhands, play cards, and tell stories.
8:00 P.M.	Get to sleep. It's another early day tomorrow!

Cowhands on many ranches still practice the old cowhand ways. Sitting around a campfire in the evening is one of them. They might even sleep under the stars. ▼

SONGS ON THE RANGE

You probably know a lot of old cowhand songs. Do you know "Home on the Range," "Red River Valley," or "The Old Chisolm Trail"? These are the songs that cowhands sang long ago.

Ranch Hands

Some cowhands work on a ranch, but instead of riding horses, they drive trucks. They are called ranch hands. They take care of the ranch. They check the grass and the health of the soil.

Ranch hands might need to build new fences and repair old ones. They keep the **windmills** working, too. Windmills are used to pump water from the ground. Cattle, horses, and wildlife need this water to survive.

These ranch hands are repairing a fence on the ranch.
▼

GOOD WORK!

Ranch hands work to be sure the land is healthy so the cattle and wildlife will have enough to eat.

Rodeo Cowhands

Rodeo is one of the biggest sports in the United States, with over 500 events each year. They show off the cowhands' skills, strength, and daring.

How is a rodeo cowhand's life different from a ranch cowhand's life? Early cowhands used to compete against one another to see who had the best herding skills on the ranch. It is the rodeo cowhand who does this now. These competitions developed into the rodeo that we know today. Rodeo cowhands compete in an arena in front of an audience.

Rodeo cowhands spend their days practicing for competitions. They practice calf roping, steer wrestling, saddle bronc riding, bareback bronc riding, bull riding, and barrel racing. Both cowboys and cowgirls compete in these games. Cowgirls also have rodeo queen competitions.

GOOD SPORTS!

Rodeo cowhands are skilled like ranch cowhands, but they are also athletes and entertainers.

Like ranch cowhands, rodeo cowhands must be ready to work, rain or shine. They can't skip their practices when it is too hot or rainy. They compete no matter what the weather is like.

RANCH AND RODEO

Early cowhands called the roundup a *rodeo*. Today's rodeo is a show and competition. Cowhands show off their skills and have contests against one another to show what they can do. The contest skills are the same ones that ranch cowhands use every day when herding the cattle.

There is so much for a cowhand to do. Do you think you could do this job?

Glossary

bandana—a scarf worn around the neck, used to protect the mouth and nose from dust or sun

brand—a registered or recognized symbol or character to indicate ownership

branding iron—a long-handled metal rod with a stamp at one end, used for branding livestock, especially cattle

cattle drive—when cowhands herd cattle to bring them together or back to the ranch

chaps—the leather leggings worn over pants to protect a cowhand's pants and legs

chuck wagon—a movable kitchen that can follow cowhands across the range

cowboy—a term for a male cowhand that was not common until the 1860s

dehorn—to remove the horns from cattle

drag men—cowhands who control the rear of the herd during a cattle drive

ear tag—to clip a tag to an animal's ear to identify it or to give it special medicine that protects it from insects

immunize—to give a shot to an animal (or person) to prevent a disease

lariat—a long rope used to catch livestock

point riders—cowhands that lead the herd during a cattle drive

range—a large, open area of grassy land where cattle move around

rodeo—an exhibition featuring cowboy skills (such as riding and roping)

scoop—a tool used by cowhands to remove the horns of cattle at a young age

stampede—a wild rush or flight of frightened animals

startle—to disturb suddenly, surprise, or alarm

swing men—cowhands who control the middle of a herd during a cattle drive

vaqueros—the Spanish word for cowhands or cowboys; the first cowhands

windmills—water pumps that use the wind to bring water up from the ground

Index